One Liners

One Liners

by Alma Heaton

This book is not an official publication of The Church of Jesus Christ of Latter-day Saints.

ISBN: 1-55517-353-5

10 9 8 7 6 5 4 3 2 1

Published and Distributed by:
925 North Main, Springville, UT 84663 • 801/489-4084
CFI
Publishing and Distribution Since 1986
Cedar Fort, Incorporated
CFI Distribution • CFI Books • Council Press • Bonneville Books

Cover design by Lyle Mortimer
Page layout by Corinne A. Bischoff
Printed in the United States of America

Table of Contents

Atten - Shun!

Before you can get attention you should know how to pay attention. We use our memory every minute of every day; every time we speak, drive a Car, or move, it requires a little thought.

Regeneration of a fading memory is within our power. Keeping your memory in top form is similar to keeping your body in shape.

Turn the task of memorizing into a creative adventure. Start by memorizing a page of these one liners. As you read, check the one liners you want to remember. The art of memory is the art of attention. When we cannot remember a one liner it is because we did not pay attention. William James wrote, "Habit diminishes the conscious attention with which our acts are performed."

People commonly turn off their minds when they are performing habitual actions. When anything is automatic, information has no way of entering your mind. To combat this observation, think of what the one liner means. Read it again then close your eyes and repeat it aloud. In this way the one liner will stand out in your mind and be included in your memory.

Memory and learning are not far apart. Try to remember lines that have the same meaning or connections. One line will then make you think of another. The line that means the most to you is the easiest to remember. When you are going to sleep at night think of the one liner and your subconscious mind will help you remember. Association is the key. When I want people to remember my name I tell them to think of turning on the heat.

Acknowledgments

I want to give credit to those people who had the original thought. The words have probably been changed through the years, but the thought is still theirs, and the unknown author needs to be thanked.

Someone said there is nothing new in the world, but it's the "sauce" and different way of serving that makes it appetizing. Council-like, water takes the shape of the container into which it is poured.

Since words do not always give the same meaning to every person who reads them, they can at least inspire meaning to those who have had similar experiences.

Introduction

For the past fifty years I have carried a small notebook with me. When I hear a capsule statement, I write it down. Now that I have retired, I have time to compile these statements under a lecture capsule. You have the book in your hand, so start now enjoying the thoughts expressed here. You will often agree with me — and sometimes disagree. But remember that smiles beat frowns, and you are in charge. No one can make you upset if you don't want them to.

I

ACTIVITY

Enthusiasm is an outward conviction of your beliefs.

We are born with genes that are ready performance.

People expected so much of me I could not disappoint them.

We are all stars — we just don't know it.

A cross-eyed discus thrower doesn't set records, but he keeps the crowd active.

To start a fire, rub two boy scouts together.

Sign on the ceiling of the wrestling room: If you can read this, you're beat.

Don't use a funeral march to radiate enthusiasm.

If you know the answer, raise your right hand. If not, raise your left. Be active.

Many people die with their music in them — I must have lots of music in me; none of it has ever come out.

We will soon have machines to play all our games.

Jesus went about doing good; some of us are just going about.

Roses are red, violets are blue, horses that lose are made into glue.

Parents should go to a child's party to see how the Sunday School lessons are absorbed into their lives.

Testimony: Girl said, "We are thankful for all the blessings we have _____." She could not think of received, so she said given. Was she wrong?

When you apply your social life to your religion it is called *living your religion.*

George Washington lost more battles than he won.

The only heaven we have is that which we make for ourselves.

All brought buckets to put out the church fire. The bishop said, "I haven't seen you in church for 30 years." "The church has not been on fire for 30 years."

"I understand you Mormons don't drink, smoke, or party." "We don't have time."

Judge said, "Why did you let the little guy beat up on you?" "I didn't want to get involved."

Recreation builds the gap between adults and youth.

A dream cannot be realized until we awake.

The only time we should go backwards is when we are rowing.

Things don't just happen; they are made to happen.

Happy people are the only ones that can open the door to the pearly gates.

If you hold a feather to a sleeping person's nose and it flutters, he's still not active.

He hit me, then ran. I never saw anyone run so fast. Then he hit me again.

I'm not going to pray for you. Three things a man should do for himself: make love, say his own prayers, blow his own nose.

You cannot teach others how to play unless you are a player yourself.

President Benson has 5 billion people to warn before the Lord comes.

Bloom where you are planted.

Leadership is coaxing those sitting on the side to stand up.

A spiritual experience is not on a peak but down in the valley.

He who picks up one end of the stick picks up the other.

When you smile you rise above the animal kingdom.

Little red hen was converted to the church and asked "will you help."

You have to be on higher ground to lift someone up.

Happiness is not what you take but what you give.

The main purpose in life is to learn how to live happily.

The problem of being punctual is that no one is there to appreciate it.

We live slightly above the animals — live beyond necessity, enjoy the arts.

A man died in High Priests' meeting. Paramedics carried three out before they found the dead man.

The best of all the travelers is not the one who tells you but the one who shows you .

The tree that never had to fight for sunshine was never good timber.

We are not judged by failures but successes.

A pipe wrench only works in one direction.

After the speaker's introduction, he said, "I feel like the donkey that was entered in the Kentucky Derby."

Talents were to help the church. I am frustrated because I have no chance to help my church.

Every year a world's record is broken — no one knows the limit.

After God said, "Well done, thou good and faithful servant," he asked, "What is my next assignment?"

How do I know you are there? I'll build you a rainbow.

The stronger the wind, the better the trees.

Activity and retention are the basis for conversation.

You're telling one thing with your voice and another with your face.

The reason for the *physical* is to develop the *spiritual.*

In case of fire, work faster.

Don't wait for things to happen. Be a part of those things that are happening.

The arts will help us keep active during the millennium.

Stay alive physically, and you can stay alive spiritually.

The temple is where you prove by your actions you have learned the lesson.

Are we going to spend eternity watching and listening?

A B C = Action Brings Change.

Those that did not help Noah build the ark got wet.

Too much sunshine makes a desert.

Before students drop out of school, they drop out of school activity.

Your future is limited only by your dreams.

Old dancers never die nor do they have the grace to fade away.

Death is an enemy because the body is separated from the spirit.

I am what I am because of what I do when I have nothing to do.

Call activity lesson correlation lesson.

A lecturer is somebody that is paid to speak in somebody's sleep.

It takes as much to save a dead men as it does to save the living.

There are two types of people on earth: those active in the church and those that ought to be.

The Lord lets us work out our own salvation because we are all different.

Sunday is the happiest day of my life because I enjoy myself. The purpose of developing talents is joy.

God cannot convert us unless we participate in the process.

We learn a skill by imitating a performance.

The great struggle is determining a balance between words and action.

Put a little laughter in your disaster.

Your painting is BEST when I criticize it MOST.

If the meek are to inherit the earth, they must be more aggressive.

You discover more about a person in one minute of play than an hour of conversation.

We teach the body so the body can teach the spirit.

Do not substitute words for actions.

Why do the requirements for awards involve activities? Why can't we just listen?

There is no growth on the comfort level.

LIFE

L — for Love

I — for Inspiration

F — for Faith

E — for Enthusiasm

All of history can be summed up in man's search for happiness.

We all want health, wealth, happiness, and enough time to enjoy all three.

You can't stick the sign of the gospel in the sand and expect the youth to read.

Inspiration, application, demonstration, revelation, dampened with a little perspiration will help you reach your destination.

While more want seats in the grandstand, fewer want to sweat it out on the field.

People don't want to burden freedom.

I wish I only had one groove in which to travel.

Happiness to the spirit is the result of what the body does to it.

Activity unlocks the mystery between the spirit and the body.

Did you come to BYU to learn or have fun? They are closely associated.

Pick yourself up one more time than you are knocked down.

Are you willing to accept the challenge to be more than you are?

WHAT:	**Change my life?**
WHY:	**Happiness.**
WHEN:	**Now.**
WHERE:	**Here.**
HOW:	**Through activity.**

People get their first glimpse of the gospel through activity.

Your spirituality is commensurate with your church activity.

Narrow way is made wider through music, drama, dance, and speech.

True leisure is not idleness. Church work is done in your leisure time.

Leisure helps us bridge the time between work and retirement.

Be active, be social, be accomplished, be interested, be prepared.

When the grand scorer writes your name, it's not that you won or lost but how you played the game.

A chapel without a cultural hall is like trying to cut with one blade of the scissors.

A lot of time would be saved if part of the time in hurrying was not wasted.

Church service begins on Monday.

Competition does not motivate unless we have a chance to win. Hope challenge is the formula.

Be *Doers*, not *Viewers*.

A sign on the door of opportunity reads "PUSH."

Love will overlook anything except being overlooked.

Here I am underground. How I wish I'd worked harder when the ground was under me.

The side of life we see is the side we show.

Work with the hand when the heart is tired.

The hand, the heart, and the head form a triangle that can bring untold happiness if used together.

Many people never let go of their own hands long enough to feel the public pulse.

For every person that is worn out, there are a hundred who have rusted out.

It is the roughness of the grindstone that sharpens the ax and the trouble in one's life that gives him a sharp edge.

The best way to throw dice is to throw them away.

B-active. B-social. B-accomplished.
B-interested. B-prepared.

It isn't what happens to our lives but what we do with what happens.

Without spiritual activity, man's life would be void. Without mental activity, man's life would numb. Without physical activity, man would be a vegetable.

Songs and laughter lubricate the biological clock.

If I tell you, you will forget. If I show you, you will remember. If I have you do it, you will understand.

A grapefruit is a lemon that had its chance and took it.

Worry is like a rocking chair. It gives you something to do, but it won't get you anywhere.

We judge others by what we are capable of doing. Others judge us by what we have done.

To look is one thing, see another, understand another, learn another; but to act on what you learn is all that matters.

There are no words that can express my appreciation, but there are actions.

The difference between a guy in a mud puddle and a geyser is enthusiasm.

Keep faith alive by keeping it active.

The great end of knowledge is performance.

If a man would kindle the life of others, he must himself glow.

Why let the world dance by when it's so easy to take the first step.

Jesus said, "I am a carpenter."

The Bugler did not know how to sound retreat, so the Colonel won the war.

Activity is magnifying our calling.

Life itself can't give you joy unless you really will it;

Life just gives you time and space; it's up to you to fill it.

Any old fish can float downstream, but takes a live fish to swim upstream.

One should never be discouraged by small beginnings.

II

BUSINESS

Opportunity is where preparation and hope meet.

Every big business starts in an attic or a basement.

I was immunized through failures.

When you enter a shower of opportunity, take off your raincoat.

Appreciate information so bad you will use it.

Do we plan like a pinball, bounce around until we get back to where we started?

We can't find a solution to a problem until we know what the problem is.

Behind every great man there is an amazed woman.

Two salesmen went to Africa to open a shoe store. One wrote home and said, "No one wears shoes." The other said, "Let's open a store as soon as we can."

Thanks for that introduction. I wrote it myself.

I despise the guys who criticize and minimize the other guys whose enterprise has made them rise above the guys who criticize.

You are a walking miracle. You have become somebody. You are a success.

Don't waste time experimenting in areas that have already been discovered.

Hundreds of ways to make money but only one honest way. What's that? I knew you wouldn't know.

You will be the richest man in the cemetery.

Wouldn't you like to live better? I don't live as good as I know now.

Do you love life? Then don't waste time for that is what life is made of.

You get the job because you listen to criticism.

Time is the coin of your life. It is the only coin you have. Only you can determine how it is spent. Be careful lest other people spend it for you.

Are you equipped to handle failure?

We enjoy taking you to Reno. We hope you enjoy being taken.

Do you think I would try to sell you a lamp in the daytime?

People can work for fifty years without having a new idea.

Call the meeting at 4:30 Friday, and people are more likely to agree with you.

We can train to control. We lose influence by using power.

As long as you are a part of an institution, do not condemn it.

Thou shalt have a sense of humor. Do not open the office without a smile.

The only way to get more in this world is to do more with the quota of ability allotted to you.

The easiest way to get to the top is to get to the bottom of things.

Stuffed shirts come in all sizes.

There are two valid reasons why some people don't mind their own business — they haven't any mind, or they haven't any business.

It isn't the load that breaks you down; it's the way you carry it.

Overestimating your ability may lead you to a fall, but underestimating it robs you of the nerve to make a start.

What a tangled web we weave when first we practice to deceive.

When things go wrong, don't go with them.

Tact: the ability to close your mouth before somebody else wants to.

A man should be like tea — his real strength appearing when he gets in hot water.

Adjust yourself to what is; do not keep trying to adjust everything else to your own desires.

Don't be so busy thinking what you are going to say that you fail to listen to what others are saying.

Tragedy is not reaching your goal but having no goal to reach.

We have no more right to consume happiness without producing it than to consume wealth without producing it. *—George Bernard Shaw*

There are many wrong ways of doing a right thing; but there never was a right way of doing a wrong thing.

Learn to obey before you command. *—Solon*

These trying times are the good old days we will be longing for a few decades hence.

You will become as small as your controlling desire; as great as your dominant aspiration.

Whatever we conceive well we express clearly.
—Nicholas Boileau

It is not always the squarest men that move in the best circles.

Men have two objects in life: to become rich, and the other richer.

Many a man has won success with a captivating smile and glad handshake.

If we were more careful of where we stepped, those that follow would not tumble.

The man with the worst reputation is most afraid of having it injured.

No need of wasting conversation on the man that won't listen to clean-cut facts.

Some men divide their time equally: one half making promises, the other half making excuses.

There's many a good thing lost for not asking for it.

Many men look through their "I's" but see themselves only.

Figures don't lie, but liars can and will they figure.

When a man gets down, fellows pounce on him like a wolf.

There is nothing new in the world; it's the sauce and different way of serving that makes it appetizing.

Do what you are expected to do — then some. It's the 'then some' that gets your wages raised.

Those that have the least to worry over worry the most.

If you want the thing done right and quickly, go to a busy man.

A loafer is an abomination, but a man busy doing nothing is worse than a loafer.

There are two classes in this world: those who say *"I can't"* and those who say *"I can."*

Many a person looks good on the outside but so does a sugar-coated pill.

Let the geese hatch before you kill the goose that lays the golden egg.

Curiosity is a whirlpool which has drained many an investor down to perdition.

To get his wealth, he spent his health; then with might and main, he spent his wealth to get his health again.

Making money and making love are just alike: the more you get, the more you want.

You can't tell what's on the inside of a man by looking on the outside.

The more a man finds fault, the more proof he hasn't done anything worthwhile himself.

There is a big difference between imitating a good man and counterfeiting him.

It's no satisfaction to have a lemon presented to us with a beautiful line of conversation.

When you fail to prepare, you prepare to fail.

The gobbler doesn't spread his tail feathers when his head is falling on the block.

When in doubt, lead a trump. This refers to business as well as cards.

Be in business with a man to know him and in love with a woman to know her.

When will man quit chasing material things and seek mental pleasures.

Poor boy, rich man; Rich son, poor grandson. This is the way the world evens things up.

Fate is very kind; every worthless man gets along far better than he should.

The faster you go the more chance you have to stub your toe.

Good manners are what you use to sometimes conceal what you were thinking.

People who spend too much time trying to play their cards right are apt to get lost in the shuffle.

There's no sense in advertising your troubles. There's no market for them.

Perseverance is a virtue, but sticking to your guns when you're out of bullets is terrible.

Why is it you very seldom see a smile on a millionaire's face?

The has-been wears shiny clothes instead of shiny shoes.

Take ten minutes at the end of each day sizing up your actions of the day.

Why is it some men who otherwise are sensible will waste time in lawsuits?

Two things to worry about: things you can control and things you can't control. Fix the first and forget the second.

The easiest way to get to the top is to get to the bottom of things.

When success turns a man's head, it always leaves him looking in the wrong direction.

If the grass is greener on the other side, the water bill is higher.

Nothing gives a person more leisure than being on time for appointments.

He who marries for money earns it.

The Lord had me fail ten businesses before I found the one he wanted me in.

The bishop would not have to be a crank if we were self-starters.

My wallet has a digestive system.

Life is but a succession of todays; thou canst not change yesterday.

What job are you preparing for? The job isn't in existence yet.

No lions are ever caught in a mousetrap.

Take ten minutes at the end of each day sizing up your actions of the day.

Each man can interpret another's experience only by his own.

III

EXPERIENCE

Experience is a wonderful thing; it helps you recognize a mistake when you make it again.

Experience is the hook we hang our words on. If you want to increase a child's vocabulary, increase his experience.

Law of the ECHO: it all comes back to you .

I do not have to duck your head under water for you to have the experience.

When I grew up, all arrows were pointing in the same direction.

Choose your ruts carefully. You will be in them for the next eight miles.

What do I get with this speeding ticket? If you get three, you get a bicycle.

When you are lost, give the horse the reins.

Criminals are tracked down by habits, not by looks.

You can't teach something you don't know any more than you can go back to a place you have never been.

Don't shackle yourself with past mistakes.

All I can do is talk about my experience. What you receive is words.

Base your testimony on your own experience. I lived its principles; I know it works. I felt its influence. I can testify. My job is to make hearers into doers.

Words should paint a picture, but words cannot unless the experience is there first.

Experience has taught me that whenever anything is on the tip of my tongue, I should keep it there.

Each man can interpret another's experience only by his own. —*Thoreau*

Knowledge is awareness of the fact that fire will burn; wisdom is remembrance of the blister.

The man who persists in doing others often terminates his career by doing time.

The darkest hour is just before dawn. If you don't believe it, ask a man that's made a night of it.

Experience is the compound extract of the result of butting in.

We say a man failed. The fact is, his business failed. He is better off for the experience.

Many great men have learned much about classics and figures, but they are shy on experience.

'Tis better to tell the truth and run than to lie and get caught in the act.

If you don't learn from your mistakes, there is no sense in making them.

If I could sell my experiences for half what they cost me, I could retire now.

In the footprints of the sands of time some people leave only the mark of a heel.

Children are not afraid to make mistakes.

Clothes may not make the man, but they show what's inside.

Edison found 100 ways that did not work.

Goofballs are well-named.

Some people speak from experience; others, from experience, don't speak.

Some people are like goats — always butting in.

A gem cannot be polished without friction, nor a man without trials.

I often quote myself. It makes the conversation interesting.

Learn from the mistakes of others. You can't live long enough to make them all yourself.

You can't describe it until you have experienced it.

Some dresses keep everyone warm but the wearer.

IV

FAMILY

Make a house a home. Love inside, be as a guide, happy and sweet.

If you could have chosen your father, what kind of a father would you have?

I can choose what kind of father my children will have.

I can't choose your life's mate, but I can put you in the right pasture.

Are you married? I was born in captivity.

Your parents don't want you to repay them.

When your lawn is worn out, ask, "Would you have had it otherwise?"

I always enjoyed a good funeral.

Make your earthly home a pattern for your heavenly home.

Get organized. Talk to wife. Get reorganized. Talk to wife. Abandon entire idea. Talk to self.

The first reunion ended with a war in heaven.

We have two handkerchiefs: one for show, one for blow.

Things that matter most happen within the walls of your own home.

This watch was given to me by my father to help me remember home.

Children, your parents prayed to your Father in Heaven to send them His best spirits.

Why did Bobby love his dog more than his father? He had more fun with his dog.

When I do something wrong, I have my children punish me.

If you're on one side of the Grand Canyon and your children on the other side, you don't talk about closing the gap.

Even the Apostleship can't compensate for failure in the home.

If we dam off a child's creative talents, they will break out in another place.

Mother can bawl you out with her eyebrows.

Zsa Zsa Gabor said, "I am a good housekeeper. Every time I get a divorce, I keep the house."

There would be no need for marriage counselors if women would quit showing their worst side to their better half.

Parents helping their children will never have time to get in trouble.

Today's definition of a family: two or more people that share resources and live together.

We need to do things for our children that they cannot do for themselves.

Make your father happy by becoming like your mother.

If it weren't for Family Home Evening, I'd never find time to talk to my children.

I live my life over in my sons.

More children are punished for imitating their parents than disobeying them.

Husbands are like fireplaces. Unattended, they go out.

My wife has a problem: she talks to herself. Mine does, too. She thinks I'm listening.

In the home you can strengthen the fiber of the nation.

Dad, is my poor report card the result of heredity or environment?

The couple was so poor they had to put the baby in the box the TV came in.

Your greatest contribution will be in the family you raise.

Only those that are united as a family will have the same feeling at family reunions.

Time will come when the only peace is in your heart and home.

Son, what do you see on this card? Three A's. Father saw only the C's.

It's a wise father who knows as much as his own son.

Parents must not only give their children a choice, but a rich background of experience from which to choose.

We are just one generation from extinction. Don't teach your children for one generation and Christianity would become extinct.

Adam and Eve left the Garden of Eden for two reasons: family and knowledge.

My progenitors paid a big price for my being here today.

I was fortunate enough to be this great man's son.

I am so grateful to you for making my life a life of happiness.

If a child always loses and a parent always wins, the problem is still not solved.

God could not be everywhere, so he created fathers.

Pressure is external; motivation is internal. I won until my boys grew up.

You must be a mould to your children.

The honeymoon is over when the dog brings your slippers and your wife barks at you.

Those who say you can't take it with you never saw a car packed for a vacation trip.

If you don't want your children to hear what you're saying, pretend you're talking to them.

Some of the new bathing suits are just big enough to keep the wearers from being tanned where they ought to be.

We have everything God has in miniature — a family.

Children who behave like little acorns can grow up to real nuts.

Hunt for the good points in your partner. Remember he has to do the same with you.

The first sure symptoms of heart and pleasure are found at home.

Very few divorce courts show very few divorces asked for in families of three or more children.

You know that wild life has turned to home life when you see more paint on the old place and less paint on the young face.

The man who has nothing to brag about but his ancestry is like a potato plant: all the good is underground.

Many a life has been wasted by parents' preferences and false estimates of the child's talents.

THE FAMILY THAT SMOKES TOGETHER

CHOKES TOGETHER

Take want from a child's life and you take away the greatest desire for living.

The prodigal son is the young man who loses everything except his way home.

It's surprising how well a homely man looks in a picture.

There's nothing wrong with teenagers that reasoning won't aggravate.

A child should not get his first experience through a lecture.

Half the population of America was under twenty when we won our freedom.

Alimony — bounty on the meeting.

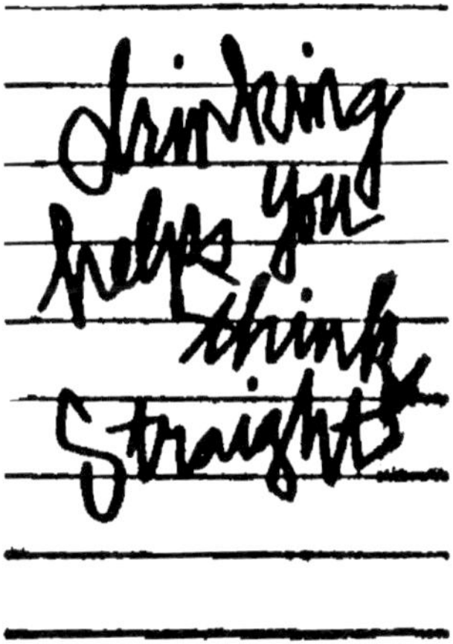

Drinking helps you think straight.

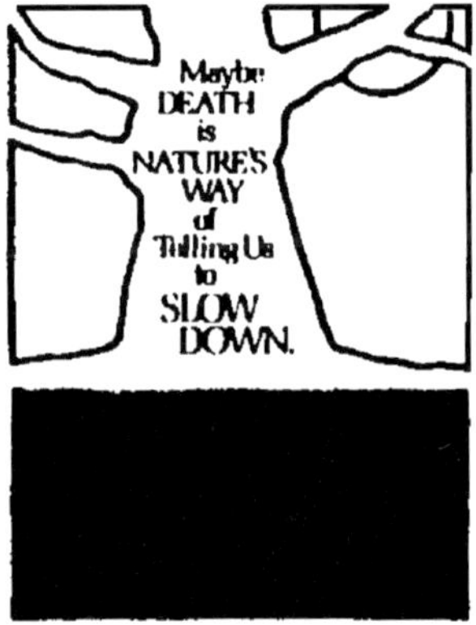

Maybe death is Nature's way of telling us to slow down.

V

Health

The poor man dances the double shuffle, glad he is alive. The rich man has rheumatism because he doesn't exercise.

It is sometimes as dangerous to be run into by a germ as by a trolley car.

Those who do not feel pain seldom think that it is felt.

If you wish to grow thinner, diminish your dinner. —*Sanders*

A rolling stone gathers no fat.

New deodorant vanishing cream — it makes you vanish and you wonder where the smell is coming from.

Opening song: Did you air the room you left this morning?

If I had known I was going to live this long, I would have taken better care of myself.

A sound mind in a sound body is the shortest description of a happy life.

General Grant was so happy when General Lee surrendered, he got out of a sick bed Happiness makes us well.

He had a firm chin, but lately the firm has taken on a couple of partners.

Please don't eat the daisies. They've been sprayed.

Sex is not a spectator sport.

When you're No. 2, you try harder.

Get really stoned. Drink wet cement. —*Sanders*

Alcohol is its own punishment.

Smokers have everything: cancer, emphysema, heart disease.

To kill a mockingbird, blow smoke on it.

"Alcohol" — the All American cop-out.

A man's venom poisons himself more than his victim. —*Sanders*

If you go long enough without a bath, even the fleas will let you alone. —*Ernie Pyle*

Every day a tree filters enough air for one person to breathe.

It is better to find a whole worm than only half of one.

Speed kills. Don't meth around.

Hunger can cause pain.

Leaf it alone!

Smoke and make your doctor rich.

Alcohol can make you sick to your liver.

Fat will grow on you.

Maybe death is nature's way of telling us to slow down.

Winston is for real: real cancer, real emphysema, real heart attacks.

LURK — something you can taste, cough after cough.

COOL — the longer you smoke, the more you choke …cough and be cool.

A cigarette named True Blue is like a prostitute named Snow White.

Be true to your teeth and they won't be false to you.

Pot smokers are like matches — they lose their heads when they light up.

Drinking helps you hit the nail squarely on the thumb.

When it comes to helping someone, junkies stop at nothing.

Smoke, choke, croak.

Diet tip — button your lip.

Smoking makes you real gone about eight years sooner.

How is a smoker like a drain? He gets choked up.

Too much food creates a great waist.

Beware of the rolling stoned.

The only way for a rich man to be healthy is to live as if he were poor.

You don't get ulcers from what you eat — but rather from what eats you.

The normal condition is happiness; worry is the result of an artificial condition.

When a man tries to drown his troubles, he thinks they are in his stomach.

Does advanced civilization mean we commence worrying at an earlier age?

Cut that out is a slang phrase borrowed evidently from doctors.

We need pebbles, glass, and grit in a gizzard. It helps digest the good stuff.

Nervousness is found among people who have nothing to do.

Alma says, "In the daytime I'm too busy to worry and at night I'm too sleepy."

Chinese pay their doctors only when they are well. They dock the doctors when they are sick.

A man's venom poisons himself more than his victim.

I drink to make other people interesting.

To laugh is to be free from worry.

There's no such thing as an easy diet — they all make you fight every inch of the weigh.

Did you ever have the measles, and, if so…how many?

VI

LOVE

We are the happiest when we are loved and when we love. Since Jesus loves us, we are joined to the greatest source of love on earth.

There isn't one person on this earth that I couldn't put my arms around and say I LOVE YOU.

You prayed for me to come, Dear. Now what do you want?

Please don't come too close; I get shesick.

Steel will rust away, but true love will last forever.

The greatest cause of divorce today is marriage.

Before we can do much more, we will have to get a better grade of prisoners.

To follow you I can't be content until I know which way you went.

Our Father in Heaven prepared us to leave home.

The Lord sends righteous children to wicked parents and wicked children to righteous parents.

What makes the lamb love Mary so? Because Mary loves the lamb, you know.

If you sit under the apple tree, I'll worm the truth out of you.

Place two electric fans facing. Start one: the other runs backwards.

I had a horse that said, "Don't fence me in." He got out and ate poison grain and died.

I want a girl just like the girl that married Richard Burton.

Happy people are the only ones that can open the door to the Pearly Gates.

You're twice as good as what I expected.

Don't tell God you love Him. Show Him.

Couples prepare for eternity by being together twenty-four hours a day.

I'm like Samson. After he lost his hair, he could not hurt anyone.

When these people see your actions, they do not believe my words.

Two horses stood head to tail. They were brushing the flies off each other's head.

The Lord was the general contractor in our home.

It is not our toughness that keeps us warm, but our tenderness.

One year of quality time is worth fifty years of emptiness.

Don't tell me you love me. Show me.

Pray for me, help me, and try to make me the man you think I am.

Be so happy your wife will want you forever.

We could have cleaned the house, but we flew kites instead.

No man is an island. Everyone's joy is my joy. Their sorrow is my sorrow.

Money's only measurement is measured by the amount of joy it brings your friends.

Black Sheep reporting on family at a reunion: all but one told of religious experiences.

Dedicate and set your home apart for the purpose of receiving spirits from God.

Make a friend each day, and you will never be lonely.

If you will all turn, you will see your neighbor smiling at you.

I'm going to put you before a firing squad for life.

Everyone I know has made a fulfillment in my life.

I want to be happy, but I can't be happy until I make you happy, too.

Love in your heart was not put there to stay. Love is not love till you give it away.

If your wife wants to learn to drive, don't stand in her way.

To a just-married couple: Treat Gail right the first week, and you will have him eating out of your hand. That will save a lot of dish washing later on.

Treat your wife like you did in courtship days. I parked in the same place, but I could not convince the officer.

We have a 50-50 marriage. I tell her what to do; she tells me where to go.

The purpose in life is to learn how to be happy.

Three rings: engagement ring, wedding ring, and suffer-ring.

I hope I can maintain your friendship through eternity.

Best timber grows together, not alone.

She gave five mouths resuscitation before finding the right one.

A lady caught a fish with five hooks in its mouth, so she threw it back.

If you're happy and you know it, then you really ought to show it.

Lift up hands that hang down. Speak up without speaking down.

Hearts must be broken that they might be rebuilt.

If I can see a smile on someone's face, it makes me happy.

He obeys better after his mother's funeral.

How would you feel if someone took your honey and nectar? Bees feel the same?

This marriage ends a friendship that began in childhood.

Life can be summed up in the service we give. Celestial is where people do things for others.

You don't have to hold the door open because I am a lady. It's because I am a gentleman.

Animals can tell when they are loved or hated.

George Washington valued his freedom so much he paid the army out of his own pocket.

Mother had sixty-five years of happy incompatibility.

No one can see our own beauty. Unmask the real me, and I'll share successes with others.

Would you be proud if you were remembered for your last contribution?

Lord said did you enjoy the talents I gave you when I sent you to earth. They're here in this box.

We judge others by what we see. We judge ourselves by how we feel.

A friend is someone who knows all about you and still loves you.

Thou shalt not get angry. Thou shalt love people. Compliment, not criticize.

Speak well of everyone, ill of no one.

Disinterested girl to ardent swain: "Henry, you're playing with ice!"

The tax collector must love poor people — he's creating so many of them.

The greatest pleasure of life is love, the greatest treasure is contentment, the greatest possession is health, and the greatest ease is sleep.

Although most new cars come equipped with automatic transmissions, one-armed drivers still use the conventional clutch.

Finding one of your own faults and doing something about it is better than finding a dozen of your neighbor's.

Actually, the so-called weaker sex is the stronger sex because of the weakness of the stronger sex for the weaker sex.

Perhaps the Lord denied woman a real sense of humor in order that she might love man instead of laugh at him.

A good husband is one who stands by his wife in troubles she would not have if she hadn't married him.

The wise man does not lay up treasures. The more he gives to others, the more he has for his own.

A man goes down into the grave holding in his clutched hand only that which he had given away.

You never realize how little you matter until you return after a month's vacation and a neighbor, seeing your baggage, says, "Going away?"

A smile is a curve that can set a lot of things straight.

Those who do not feel pain seldom think that it is felt. —*Samuel Johnson*

Humor is the only thing that stands between us and the dark. —*Mark Van Doren*

Visits always give pleasure. If not the coming, then the going.

Stop discrimination. Hate everybody.

There is no cure for birth and death save to enjoy the interval.

To achieve success, give freely of that which costs nothing — friendliness, sincere interest, good counsel.

Kindness is the one commodity of which you should spend more than you earn.

The greatest remedy for anger is delay.

Life's most important arithmetic lesson: Happiness multiplies by division.

A good rule for going through life is to keep the heart a little softer than the head.

A rumor is about as hard to unspread as butter.

If you would be eternally rich, invest in the human soul.

The safest way to knock the chip off a fellow's shoulder is by patting him on the back.

If your feelings are hurt, do not show it to anyone.

Win a friend by convincing him that you are his friend.

Reprove thy friend privately; commend him publicly.

Cherish your friends — without them you would be a stranger.

Your opinion of others is usually their opinion of you.

A man without mirth is like a wagon without springs.

A friend is one who laughs at your stories even if they aren't very good and sympathizes with your troubles even if they aren't so bad.

Be kind to your enemies; you made them.

I know my husband can be tender because he talks that way to the dog.

If your body is happy, notify your face.

Invest in the mind. I want to know what I did right, not wrong.

He that cloth a base thing in zeal for his friend burns the golden thread that ties their hearts together. —*Jeremy Taylor*

Man is proof enough that woman can take a joke.

Oh, if it be to choose and call thee mine, Love, thou art every day, my Valentine! —*Thomas Hood*

A thankful heart is not only the greatest virtue, but the parent of all the other virtues. —*Cicero*

The end of all learning is to know God, and out of that knowledge to love and imitate him. —*Milton*

When two quarrel, both are in the wrong.

"If you treat a man as he is, he will stay as he is, but if you treat him as if he were what he ought to be, and could be, he will become that bigger and better man." —*Goethe*

You can't have friends if you spend your time making enemies.

Don't think because a man has done you a favor he is under everlasting obligation to you.

Unless I get some happiness every day, I will never find it on any tomorrow.

When a man's own dog won't follow him, beware of that man.

Beware of any man who does not like children, dogs, music, and laughter.

Be happy, and your friends are many. Be sad, and you lose them all.

In every life there is a door marked "private."

Our faults attract more attention than our virtues.

Undertakers report that they never saw a death certificate that read "killed by kindness."

Revenge. That's the poorest compensation man ever worked for.

Never judge a man by his clothes. Many a patched pair of trousers covers an honest heart.

The ore is not beautiful, but the gold is there.

A woman can keep a secret, but she can't help but let you know she is keeping it.

There's happiness all around us, but we are generally looking way over yonder.

No lie can hurt a man for a long time.

Lies do not hurt; it's the truth that hurts.

We like to be laughed at for our wit, not for our folly.

A little word in kindness spoken, a motion or a tear, has often healed the heart that's broken and made a friend sincere.

No one ever repeated a scandalous story with a good purpose.

Your will is read after you are dead. Let love alone live. All your hate should be interred with your bones.

It will be proper to speak to each other in heaven without an introduction.

All you get out of life is board, clothes, love, and happiness. All money buys is board and clothes.

A single sister is important, she makes her married sister see how much fun a family is.

We should have less law, less lawyers, more living, and more lovers.

Give nut picks for Christmas, they are never used and will stand a monument from the giver.

Woman was the last of the creation; otherwise, she would have insisted on bossing the job.

Happiness isn't found in searching for it — it can come quietly while you are helping others.

No person can be considered a failure who has been the cause of a child's laughter.

Be pleasant every morning until ten o'clock. The rest of the day will take care of itself.

Mother: the one person in the world whose kindness was never the preface to a request.

Don't tie grass in the trail in which your brother travels.

It's asking too much to love your enemy — let's compromise and forget them.

If you can't sing, don't cause thunder — don't be a shadow in the light of love and life.

It's nice to be important, but it's also important to be nice.

The mind breaks up when love breaks down.

Powers of love should take over the love of power.

If you would be eternally rich, invest in the human soul.

You can only make others better by being good yourself.

He that can have patience can have what he will.

Love is the most powerful tool we have.

If you kicked a man for his trouble, you couldn't sit down.

Hunt for the good points in the other fellow. Remember, he has to do the same with you.

Keep your temper — no one else wants it.

You cannot whitewash yourself by blackening others.

To achieve success, give freely of that which costs nothing: friendliness, sincere interest, good counsel.

Love — the feeling that makes a boy think as much of a girl as he does of himself.

When all is said and done, it is usually she who has said it and he who has done it…

Husbands are awkward things to deal with; even keeping them in hot water will not make them tender. —*Mary Buckley*

Nothing is so full of victory as patience. —*Chinese Proverb*

Love will overlook anything except being overlooked.

Laughing is the sensation of feeling good all over but showing it in one spot.

A successful marriage requires falling in love many times, always with the same person.

I will sum up my life in terms of what service I have rendered.

Yes, man has one advantage — he can get married if he wants to.

It's nice to be important, but it's more important to be nice.

The main influences of the moon are on the tied and untied.

VII

GROWING OLDER

You don't stop playing because you grow old. You grow old because you stop playing.

Death is just another birth.

What is new comes out of what is old.

Creativity is never dead as long as spring records winter.

You are superior in some way more than any other person on earth.

Old fishermen never die; they just smell that way.

Very sorry. At my age, I can't take *yes* for an answer.

Dad died at 95 on his way to work.

M C at class reunion: It's interesting to look around and see how many of you have passed away.

My interest is in the future because that is where I'm going to spend the rest of my life.

They don't understand us 85-year-old kids. Is this a generation gap?

Growing old is like matter over mind: if you don't mind, it doesn't matter.

It's nice to look into your faces — some of them need looking into.

Whatever happened to the child that used to be me?

Tell your neighbor your nickname and how you got it.

Talking to LeGrande Richards was like talking to the Old Testament.

Between the ages of 12 and 17 parents grow 20 years.

I have become better acquainted with the deceased at a funeral than through life.

I'm glad I'm bald. When company comes, all I have to do is straighten my tie.

Laughing made me bald. It cuts off the circulation from the scalp.

Every hair of my head is numbered. Just call me chrome dome or cueball.

This is not my head. My neck is just blowing bubble gum.

My mother told me I would come out on top.

Just remember, grass does not grow on busy streets nor hair on brainy heads.

First Corinthians 11-14 says long hair is a shame unto him.

Barber says, "Come on in, Heaton. You haven't a thing to lose."

I'm not bald when I sneeze.

I went bald because I could not find a combination of Lion Hippo Crocodile and snake oil.

Bald heads are like snowflakes — no two are alike.

The Lord made very few perfect heads — others he had to cover with hair.

'Tis what you learn after you know it all that counts.

Tragedy of life is not reaching your goal but having no goal to reach.

He is not dead. He has just wandered into another era.

Now that you're old and rich, you should make a will. Now that I'm rich, I have lost interest in willing.

We have not completed our life when we come to our funeral — none of us is prepared for resurrection.

Death is not going away but coming home.

Leisure should be an opportunity, not a temptation.

Old folks know more about young folks than young folks know about old folks.

I'm not bald. I'm just growing a new face.

That which you give away remains with you forever.

We reach our peek and stay there for life.

It takes more courage to suffer than to die.

I hope when I die I find I have not lived.

You don't have to be old to be lonely.

In high school you have hair but no money; in reunions, you have money but no hair.

Dancing is not only for the young but for those who want to stay young.

Leisure assumes recreation. Recreation assumes freedom. Freedom assumes choice. Choice assumes you have the ability and intelligence to use your freedom wisely.

We are not ghosts wandering through life during retirement.

Time may be a good wound healer, but it's no good as a wrinkle remover.

The happiness of death is kept from us so we can enjoy life.

None are so old as those who live without enthusiasm.

Where have all the old smokers gone?

Stamp out old age — Smoke.

Fun is like life insurance; the older you get, the more it costs.

Make good use of your time — it's later than you think.

I have a bald head; the Lord knew who would have time to comb their hair.

The best thing to save for your old age is yourself.

The man and the cucumber are valueless when they are ripe.

Put pleasant things in our bank of life that we can draw upon in after years.

The path of duty is not as smooth as a railroad, but it always leads to the station of rest.

We do, in later years, what we learn in our youth.

Men are like beards — they do not have them until they grow up.

An adjusted person is one that can make the same mistake twice without letting it bother him.

No one grows old by living, only by losing interest in living.

Save now and live later. We mistakenly equate success by material things.

VIII

RELIGION

I'd rather see a sermon than hear one any day.

For every one that thinks about hell, 1,000 think about heaven.

God did not send us here to fail. He said, "Go down there and become a celestial being."

Tithing: I just throw my money in the air and let the Lord catch what He wants.

If you cannot trust yourself in the hands of man, trust in God.

We do not go into a game without knowing the rules.

Invited (in church) means required.

Will all who are not willing to serve the Lord stand up. Good. Then I can give an assignment.

Jesus, after resurrection, let them feel his physical body. He used physical to teach the spiritual.

Cooperate rather than compete in church.

Husband who bought a cemetery lot for his wife for their anniversary. "Next year," she said, "you forgot a gift for our anniversary." He said, "You did not use the one I gave you last year."

Courage is fear that has said its prayers.

Prayer is like shaving. No matter how well you do it, you have to do it tomorrow.

We have celestial, terrestrial, and telestial home teachers: first, middle, and end-of-the-month.

Has the church restricted you in any way?

Lady kissed all men on front row in church. She said, "Bible says to do unto others as you would have them do unto you."

A gospel that does not exalt a person here will never do it over there.

I grabbed him and said, "I think the Devil has you." He said, "I think so, too."

Only thing worse than an atheist is a man who says "I do not know."

When we make footprints in the sand of time, will it be a heel or a soul?

It was easier to go to church than answer for not going.

Spend your time in nothing that needs repenting of.

Leave your troubles outside the temple door.

Gospel makes bad men good and good men better.

Me and the Lord got together. Isn't that the shortest distance.

The Lord and I came very close when I was in the hospital.

If I had a cow, I would not feed her the whole load at one time.

Do not put question marks where the Lord puts periods.

Boy said, "I can't have fun at a dance if the Lord's there."

You have to pay for your sins. If you have already paid, disregard this notice.

It would take me all day to tell you his good points and one minute to tell you his bad points. Then I would have to make them up.

The life of every good man preaches a sermon.

When I raise my hand, sit up straight. Hand down, relax. My talk must have been satisfying because they never asked me to speak again.

You never stand taller than when you kneel to pray.

Ignorance brings bondage. Trust makes us free.

My spirit is the highest when I am driven to my knees.

I had a joke, but it was not appropriate. So I asked the bishop. Now I know two jokes that are not appropriate.

Think not what the church can do for you but what you can do for the church.

When we use underclothing for outer clothing, we are breaking church standards.

If Eve was so beautiful and Adam so handsome, why are we so ugly? Because we started raising Cain.

The fear of the Lord is the beginning of knowledge.

Youth would rather serve than be served.

Christians should be happy. They have opportunities other people never think of.

Our Father in Heaven uses all five senses. He is not hard of hearing. He speaks when we ask questions. He touches us when we feel His hand in ours. He is watching us as we fulfill our church duties. He can smell us when we perspire serving our fellow men. He uses his tongue to bless us. He places flavor in the food we eat.

What kind of a church would this be if all members were just like me?

Evil must be present in order for us to resist temptation.

Bishop is worried about our salvation; don't worry him about money.

Thou shalt not work on the sabbath day. Call it church joy instead of church work.

Comprehend blessings with sixth sense: spiritual sense.

Christians will put the *Constitution* back into operation.

Two things we can do: repent and forgive. The power is within you.

The Lord will come when we have time to hear Him.

Satan is more afraid of prayer than anything else.

Man is the only animal that searches out danger.

Satan cannot create new things; he just perverts what's here.

People cannot change truth, but truth can change people.

Temptation comes with every commandment.

You dial God by saying, Our Father which art in Heaven.

The component part of the brain is the physical part of the body in which the spirit works.

Bible is like the cover of an orange — no good till you break the cover.

God so loved the world that He did not send a committee.

Eleventh commandment: Thou shalt not take thyself too seriously.

Have joy in the temple this day. We are commanded to be happy.

My body is a temple, not a visitors' center, and you do not have a recommend.

To really feed His sheep, you need to know what to feed them.

Saint Peter asked at the Pearly Gates: Is anyone on earth better because you were there?

He went from the dark side of the moon and found this great light.

I'm to preach, you're to listen. If you get through before I do, raise your hand.

How much are you worth? Esau sold his birthright for a mess of pottage.

If you're not as close to the Lord as you used to be, guess who moved.

You were chosen before birth as Abraham to be what you are.

How would you like to be shot into space with just an instruction book on how to get back? You have the Bible.

God reveals some things to us that He does not reveal to the Prophet.

Are you dressed spiritually to meet your Father in Heaven?

Are you Jesus' mother. No, I am just one of His children.

I might speak by the Holy Ghost, but those not in tune will not bear me.

What would happen if all Latter-day Saints were active?

You are a child of God. Call home often.

Talents: You go back with more than you came with.

Meekness is gentleness. It enhances our enjoyment.

Sheep herders follow and push; shepherds lead and pull.

When I pass the church, I pay a visit. Then when they carry me in feet first the Lord won't say, "Who is it?"

We have a new world. You can go to hell faster than any other time.

The time will come when the Christian women are the only ones willing to have children.

Saving ourselves is called salvation. Saving others is called leadership.

The spirit needs air as does the body.

If you were on trial for being a Christian, would they have enough evidence to convict you?

Live so that all that know you will know Him.

Why did you play like a champion? My blind, deceased father was watching me.

We don't remember our pre-earth life because God wants us to learn to be happy here.

If this church were not here, this country would have been destroyed many times.

The power of your spirit humbles me.

This is one dispensation in which the gospel will not be taken away.

One good thing I can say about Satan: he is not lazy.

In last days every knee shall bow, but it does not say they will accept.

The Gospel is true as long as it is translated correctly.

If we could remember what we did in heaven, we would be religious fanatics.

Stay on your knees long enough for the Lord to answer.

If ever the world needed religion, it needs it now.

You cannot be honest with God unless you are honest with yourself.

I did the right thing for the right reason.

I would rather be a deacon in the church than a king in any country.

What we are after here is what we are here after.

The Lord does not cause accidents, but He uses accidents to teach lessons.

If there were no restrictions, we would become like the Romans and lose our freedom.

The Lord has a dance program because the worldly dances did not please Him.

If you're not sure of church standards, ask your bishop.

The kingdom is made up of those who live the gospel, not just know it.

There are 35,000 laws made up to enforce the Ten Commandments. If you have grown too big for the church, you have the "don't care" attitude.

God made me as I am for a special purpose.

Purpose of body is to feed the spirit. If you're happy, tell your face. Show me you love me.

People will not come to a meetinghouse on how to improve the town, but all will come to watch it burn.

Work is what a Christian used to do in his free time.

The road to ruin is always in good repair. The travelers pay for it.

The Lord does not want to come to a people who have no time to listen to Him.

When life gets easier physically, it gets harder morally.

Pretense is being active in the church but not in the gospel.

The greatest commandment for you is the one you have the hardest time living.

We do not serve in our name but in the name of our Savior.

The Lord did not say, "Get a pencil and paper; I'm going to give you a revelation."

Do we spend so much time learning our religion that we do not have time to live it?

Once I was carnal; now I am spiritual.

We came to this earth to learn something we once knew.

A veil is drawn over our brain, but our spirits want to go back.

There are several good protections against temptations. But the surest is cowardice. —*Mark Twain*

Most people don't need to be led into temptation—they find their own way.

One cannot go into a flour mill or a coal mine without being covered with the flying dust. No more can he read an evil book without leaving a stain on his memory and his soul.

If we get too broad minded, we can't travel the straight and narrow.

If we get into the highest degree of celestial glory, it will be because our actions will make us feel at home when we get there.

Some people say "Our Father" on Sunday and go around the rest of the week acting like orphans.

Fear is lack of faith, and lack of faith is ignorance.

It's easier to go to church than tell them why you did not go.

Joseph Smith: was author, translator, seer, revelator, apostle, prophet, organizer, president, leader, economist, architect, record keeper, linguist, politician, militaire.

An atheist is a man who has no invisible means of support. —*John Buchanan*

Democratic government is the political expression of Christianity.

Man is more than physical — man is spiritual, and must have daily food for his soul.

Every day is judgment day. Use a lot of it.

There is no man suddenly good or evil. The process is gradual.

The optimist makes his own heaven and enjoys it. The pessimist makes his own hell and suffers as he goes through life.

The more we speak the truth, the more we can depict the ring of truth in others.

The more we lie, the more we think others are lying.

There are mushroom men and men of oak. The church is built on the steady oak plan.

Start a new religion. Make it something you can't explain and you will have converts galore.

If angels had to live with some men, there would be a lot of fallen angels.

To leave your umbrella in church is a sure sign of Christian faith.

Many who cast their bread upon the waters expect club sandwiches back in return.

Many men figure just how far they dare to be bad.

If we are out to save souls, why do we discriminate between the good and the bad.

The most successful liar is the one who lies the least.

In church we sing. We shall know each other over there but don't try to know each other here.

Satan wants us to die early.

We do not get to heaven on what we know — but what we do.

May we fly from the temptations we cannot resist.

With some people, truth is like a girdle; it is made to be stretched.

A lie can be beautiful only when truth is ugly.

I am destroying my enemies when I make them my friends.

Satan has the same experiences we do, but he interprets them differently.

Live as if you expected to live a hundred years but might die tomorrow.

Pray as if everything depended on God; then work as if everything depended on you .

Anyone who calls a rose by any other name is probably pruning it.

A great way to find out what you want from life is to write your own epitaph.

Knowledge cannot make us all leaders, but it can help us decide which leader to follow.

The family home evening was revealed to keep the church together.

When people did not appreciate the gospel, it was taken from them. Keep faith alive by keeping it active.

We go to church to have our weekly experiences interpreted for us.

Anything that takes more time than God is your God.

Spiritual, ethical, and moral ideals will save the world — not bombs.

There are no atheists in foxholes.

Body without spirit is dead.

We suffer by our sins, not for them.

When I have something important to say, I wear my dark suit.

All revelation does not come by inspiration.

The mockingbird is like Satan's angels. He sings like other birds but lays eggs in their nests.

The greatest honor we can pay to truth is to use it.

All that is necessary for the triumph of evil is for good men to do nothing.

IX

SCHOOL

Some drink from the fountain of knowledge; others just come to gargle.

Let's not act like a student when we are a professional.

Graduates, you have reaped where others have sown.

Music and dancing are continual; watching and listening are intermittent.

Learning is like rowing upstream — not to advance is to drop back.

Government average is when you stand with one foot in a bucket of boiling water and the other foot in ice.

If you think they took prayer out of school, you should hear teachers before they open the school doors.

I went to class one day. I got 99% on the final test. That one day did throw me off a little.

Not what the girl can do with rhythm, but what rhythm can do for the girl that counts.

Adam, where art thou was the beginning of the first commencement.

If our education does not change us, it is not doing us any good.

Don't listen to this boy. He just goes around repeating what others say.

The only thing more costly than education is ignorance.

Each student in class is in some way superior to the teacher.

A real teacher cannot be duplicated but can only be copied.

Education is not teaching you what you do not know, but teaching you how to use the knowledge you have.

Spend your money on things that will last for an eternity.

This day is a fight for the minds of men.

Preparation comes before opportunity.

You can fill a jar, but the human mind can never be filled.

People believe more of what they see than what they hear.

Put your head under water. When you want to learn as much as you want air, see me.

Meeting parents who send children to college makes me work harder to educate them.

Students did not come to school by accident.

Some students come to BYU as a last chance to hold onto their faith.

Knowledge can make you a clever devil.

Everything you know you have learned from others.

In order to teach, you have to be teachable.

L — ove.
E — xample.
A — ction.
D — esire.
E — nthusiasm.
R — esponsible.
S — elf-control
H — umility.
I — nspire.
P — ersonality.

My greatest teachers did not know they were influencing my life at the time.

Don't say you're not so hot. Say you're cool. Don't say you're lazy. Say you lack self-esteem.

Next best thing to knowing something is knowing where to find it.

Education is the process of passing notes of teachers to notes of pupils without going through the heads of either.

I have 50,000 students out there making me a celestial billionaire.

Roses are red, violets are blue. She copied my paper, and she flunked, too.

Great things are accomplished by two people—those smart enough to know it can be done, and those so dumb they don't know it cannot be done.

Things to learn doubles every year.

Teenage years are critical: you decide on education, your vocation, a mission, and you fall in love.

We receive the true meaning when we read it the second time.

You should be both teacher and pupil. There is no one to check up on you.

No longer parents send letters to teachers. You are the guardian, too.

Matrimony: an institution of learning in which a man loses his bachelor's degree and his wife acquires a master's.

Knowledge like timber is best when well seasoned.

Laugh and the class laughs with you, but you stay after school alone.

Any complex subject becomes elementary the instant it is understood.

A college education seldom hurts a man if he's willing to learn a little something after he graduates.

Great books are the great souls which have left the bodies of great beings and have come to talk with us.

Real intelligence is a creative use of knowledge, not merely an accumulation of facts.

The price of education is great — but not nearly so great as the price of ignorance.

Since time began, the ten fingers of a man have been his best friends.

Your best may be better than my best. He gets a hundred whether the best is great or small.

What did you learn today? Not enough; I have to go back tomorrow.

Silence is eloquent as a thunder bolt when your teacher looks at you and speaketh not.

Minds are like parachutes; they only function when open.

Five senses — too many people touch without feeling, eat without tasting, breathe without smelling, look without seeing, listen without hearing.

The will to learn is called readiness.

The dictionary is the only place where success comes before work.

A highbrow is a person educated beyond his intelligence.

Education is forcing abstract ideas into concrete heads.

FIVE SENSES

I have five senses you must reach

If I am to learn and you are to teach.

With touch, taste, smell and sight so clear,

Why must I receive all my sense by ear?

It's more impressive if you can see what you are hearing.

Education is describing a bathing beauty without using your hands.

It's more impressive if you can see what you are hearing.

X

THINKING

You will be as good as you want to be
and no more.

We need a way to evaluate your progress.

Creativity: Write all the excuses you can from a wrecked auto.

As soon as I say "now" it becomes "then."

What I can't see is more important than what I can see.

God help them who are found helping themselves.

Do you have wagon wheels or cog wheels in your head?

We do not say the nastiest things in the nicest way.

If you want to know what I think about the 25-cent stamp — phone me.

Why does the whole audience straighten up with some speakers?

I told you an hour ago I would be there in a minute, so don't chastise me.

Is the pig or chicken a sacrifice or contribution to society?

If you don't know where you are going, any road will get you there.

The South lost the war because they dug in so deep they could not see the enemy coming.

A raised hand will keep you awake, but think of the answer first.

It's hard to put into words what's in my heart.

Nothing you say could offend me. I am in control.

We know how to scratch, but we do not know where it itches.

Everyone is entitled to my opinion.

Your foot sticks to the roof of your mouth.

We influence everyone we come in contact with.

My doctor said I could not go on a mission, so I found another doctor.

I had trouble with names until I took that course from Sam Cornage.

Missionary sign: EVERYTHING YOU WANT TO KNOW ABOUT MORMONISM BUT WERE AFRAID TO ASK.

A black balloon will go just as high. It's what's inside that makes it rise.

Skills are the basis for thinking.

This is a time for wondering, searching, and asking.

We can shorten our life or we can lengthen it.

The grass is always greener over the septic tank.

Be light-hearted, not light-minded.

When you reach up, it's easier to pull down than for them to pull up.

If it weren't for bad luck, I'd have no luck at all.

The brain is like a sink: when a new idea enters, it's all muddled up.

Bed was narrow so he put on a bedspread.

He called his girl Postscript because her name was Adeline.

He wanted to make his pants last, so he made his coat first.

Spectator is always right; he gets only one viewpoint.

When man looks back at the Twentieth Century, what will be his comments?

You're 50 percent right half the time.

He prayed, Help us to come to church the biggest share of the time.

Before I say anything, I would like to make a few remarks…

How many legs would a sheep have if you called the tail a leg? Five. Saying it doesn't make it so.

"Ore" cried Fernando as the bull tore his hide away.

With planes going faster than sound it's possible for a man to speak behind his back.

Get the clinker out of your thinker.

Why are you afraid to be happy?

Two tons of canaries in a one ton truck: beat on the side to keep half of them flying.

You choose a car according to your personality.

Some people will not take the responsibility that freedom requires.

Don't force yourself into the same mold.

Attention is the mother of memory.

Tragedy plus time equals humor.

A habit is like a bed: it's easy to get into but hard to get out of.

Use the KISS method when talking: Keep it simple, stupid.

Many times I have received unrighteous criticism.

Control your thoughts when you criticize.

Strive for wisdom, not money.

Introduction can be an obituary: they do such a good job, you would rather be dead.

Make excuses work for you not against you .

You can tell the girl's character by her clothes. Oh, she has more character than that.

Thin and fat cat standing by a mouse hole. Fat cat said, Speak their language. Bark like a dog. The mouse will know the dog will scare the cat away and will come out of the hole.

Man offered a lady his seat, and she fainted. She came to and said, "Thank you," and he fainted.

Are we doing something that demands more than animal reactions?

Thoughts are the basis of our exaltation.

In Europe the Elders translated Marie and I instead of the language.

Dad, how can I explain why things get longer with heat and shorter with cold? Summer days are longer because it's hotter. Winter days are shorter because it's colder.

A man has to be knocked senseless before he comes to his senses.

I did not leave anyone to guard the head gate before I crawled in to unplug the culvert.

It is not what we eat but what we digest that makes us strong.

Missionaries go out to heal the dead, cast out the sick, and raise the devil.

If you don't know where you are going, you don't care how fast you go.

Improve time and time will improve you.

No one has the power to hurt your feelings.

Make up your mind. Do you have to decide to get up at 8:00 o'clock every morning?

The best way to get the best of any argument is to avoid it.

Have the courage to face your faults.

Horsepower was a lot safer when the horses had it.

Though reading and conversation may furnish us with many ideas of man and things, yet our judgment must be formed through our own meditation.

It's fine to talk straight from the shoulder, but it's better to talk from higher up.

Happiness may be thought, sought, or caught, but not bought.

Next to having a great aim is to recognize the psychological moment to pull the trigger.

Some people have a veneer that comes off easily with a little alcohol.

Don't throw your mouth into high gear until you are sure your brain is turning over.

The question of the hydrogen bomb is not who is right but who is left.

Little things affect little minds. —*Disraeli*

If you are blessed with a sympathetic disposition, don't waste it on yourself.

There is no cure for birth and death save to enjoy the interval. —*Santayana*

It is a sin to be silent when it is your duty to protest. —*Lincoln*

If it weren't for the optimist, the pessimist wouldn't know how good off he wasn't.

There are some things you can't do alone.

Blow your nose, not your mind.

Man is not the creature of circumstance; circumstances are the creatures of man. —*Disraeli*

From the Redwood Forest to the Gulf Stream Oil Slick, this land was made for you and me.

Speak first, think afterwards, and repent forever.

Some students are like goats — always butting in.

Avoid that run-down feeling — look both ways before crossing.

Plan ahead — it wasn't raining when Noah built the ark.

Think for yourself. Your friends may be wrong.

If at first you don't succeed — you're only average.

A lot of open mouths should be CLOSED FOR REPAIRS.

Some students have waterproof voices—no one can drown them out.

Like water, vulgarity seeks its own level.

Most people feel young until they try to prove it.

With some people, truth is like a girdle…it's made to be stretched.

The best reformers the world has seen were those who began with themselves.

The biggest liar is one who talks most of himself.

Some folks seem to be best suited for just one job …tester in a mattress factory.

Blubber feels just like it sounds.

Blessed are those who can give without remembering and take without forgetting.

The difference between moat men is little enough — but that little makes the difference.

Most of us spend too much time letting off steam.

A whale is harpooned only when blowing off.

The superior man blames himself; the inferior man blames others.

A wise man knows everything; a shrewd man knows everyone.

A person who talks about his inferiors hasn't any.

There's a line on the ocean where, by crossing it, you can lose a day. There's a line on the highway where you can do even better than that.

Thinking is one thing that no one has ever been able to tax.

On the highway a minute saved may be a lifetime squandered.

When girls turn a man's head, it always leaves him looking in the wrong direction.

True merit is like a river; the deeper it is, the less noise it makes.

The teacher who thinks he has arrived is already slipping.

By the street of "by and by" one arrives at the house of "never."

Keep smiling. People will wonder what you are up to.

Balance fantasy with fact — dream, but also do — wish, but also build — imagine, but ever face reality.

Lives of great men all remind us we can make our lives sublime.

Strengthen your mind. Read something that requires effort, thought, and concentration.

Act courteously, criticize not one bit, and try not to improve or regulate anyone except yourself.

Keep your temper. Nobody else wants it.

It is better to be calm than clever.

Be happy. We assume that what Abraham Lincoln said is true — "Most folk are about as happy as they make up their minds to be."

Bad officials are elected by good citizens who do not vote.

The right angle to solve a difficult problem is the "Try-angle."

Keep your face to the sunshine and you cannot see the shadow.

The trouble with most arguments is that they are devoted to determining who's right rather than what.

A man may fall several times, but he isn't a failure until he starts saying someone pushed him.

Life is getting what you want; happiness is wanting what you get.

No one has ever learned anything by talking to himself.

Tolerance is the ability to keep your shirt on when you're hot under the collar.

There's nothing like the first horseback ride to make a person feel better off.

Worry is the interest you pay on trouble before you get it.

The mind, grappling with great aims and wrestling with mighty impediments, grows by a certain necessity to the stature of greatness. *—Bryant*

All women's hats are different — milliners seldom make the same mistake twice.

No really great man ever thought so himself. *—William Hazlitt*

Ideas are very much like children — your own are very wonderful.

Denying a fault doubles it.

When you encounter stumbling stones along the way, step on them and go ahead.

Distance lends enchantment but not when you're out of gas.

Give some weeds an inch and they will take the yard.

Habit is a cable; we weave a thread of it each day, and it becomes so strong we cannot break it. *—Horace Mann*

Ideas are funny things; they won't work unless you do.

When men speak ill of thee, live so as nobody may believe them. *—Plato*

This is a funny world — its wonders never cease. Civilized people are at war, and savages are at peace.

Youth's natural desire to get ahead is most noticeable on the highway.

If you have a poor memory, you can cure yourself by lending small sums to your friends.

The seed that is sown is the seed that will be harvested.

One string out of tune will spoil the music played on the best piano.

The ability to say no is more valuable to a man than the ability to read Latin.

To keep your friend's interest, don't tell him all you know the first time you meet him.

Half the lies they tell about you aren't true.

Two things to worry about when called on to talk: stand it. The other you can't think of at the present.

One wise man can fool a dozen fools easier than a dozen fools can fool one wise man.

The boat that is built for speed will not carry much weight.

Men are like fish; neither would get in trouble if they kept their mouths shut.

There is a truth about a lie. If you let it go, it will chase itself to death.

We are all fellow travelers on the same island floating through space.

Manslaughter is a penal offense. Man's laughter isn't, and it's spelled the same.

Ego-ism looks through the big end of the telescope. Egotism looks through the small end.

Grief starts on the surface, but when it bores into the soul, it's agony.

Many a man that has been sensible all his life lets a fool make a fool of him.

A fast horse can't go fast far.

Many people dance when the devil plays the fiddle and won't stop till there's fire.

A man with an idea is sometimes a bore or sometimes an inspiration. It depends on the person and the idea.

Today is the day you worried about yesterday. Cheer up and live today.

Alma says when it rains, it's good for ducks and dust; when dry, it's good for rheumatism.

You can lead a fool to talk, but you can't make him think.

An evil thought does little harm if you don't express it to listening ears.

Dogs bark at the moon, but the moon doesn't answer.

Nothing is more than half as good as it would be if it was twice as good as it is.

If everything everybody wished would happen, what a mess this world would be in.

If you want to be happy, take things as they come, and don't hold onto them as they go.

We waste too much time criticizing the faults of those whose strong points we could be praising.

What a lot of time would be saved if part of the time in hurrying wasn't wasted.

Look at that old album and see mother when she was a bride. Then think a bit.

Many an idea is a notion without a motion. You are not what you think you are, but what you think.

The best way to reach great heights is to stay on the level.

The greatest undeveloped territory lies under your hat.

Little things affect little minds.

Don't let a warm idea freeze to death.

Greater than the force of marching feet is an idea whose hour is come.

Remember, an idea does not care who has it.

The future depends on the decisions you make today.

A man's mind, when stretched by a new idea, will never go back to its original dimension.

Can you eat your own words when you are wrong, or does it turn your stomach?

Tact: ability to close your mouth before somebody else wants to.

Don't try to jump a puddle in two jumps.

A horse can't pull and kick at the same time.

The only difference between a rut and a grave is their dimensions.

A rumor is about as hard to unspread as butter.

Four things come not back: the spoken word, the sped arrow, the past life, the neglected opportunity.

Do you always believe in safety first?

Before you raise your voice, strengthen your argument.

Sparks fly when two ignorant heads clash.

The greatest of faults is to be conscious of none.

The greatest remedy for anger is delay.

Take care of the minutes; the hours will take care of themselves. *—Lord Chesterfield*

Man who stumble over same rock twice deserve to break neck. *—Chinese Proverb*

When you have nothing to say, say nothing.
—Charles Caleb Colton

Men do not stumble over mountains, but over molehills. *—Confucius*

The same heat that melts the butter hardens the egg.

Anything that gets in your way is your goal.

I answer the same question differently; it depends on your needs.

A man can't walk far going the opposite direction on top of a train.

We become what we think about.

Every man has the power to destroy himself.

Two ends: one we think with, one we sit on. Heads we win; tails we lose.

We know more about killing than we do about living.

We learn from our opponents. They point out our mistakes.

Advertisements and people are anxious to help us destroy ourselves.

Creative leisure is still master rather than a servant of time.

Put emphasis on creativity, not on conformity.

Speak to my eyes, not my ears.

Optimism is life; pessimism, slow suicide.

Our bodies are the tools by which we learn.

We have more time, less to do, and more money to do it with.

Why are we here? Because we are not all there.

Shortest distance between two dates is a good line.

Some feel mortified for having to give up a pleasure he did not want in the first place.

The reason some of us get lost in thought is because it's unfamiliar territory.

Learn something in life that outlasts life.

The man that cannot control his thoughts cannot control his actions.

Patient: I have trouble with my memory. Doctor: How long has this been going on? Patient: How long has what been going on?

Take time to listen, take time to care. If you really listen, my mind is yours to share.

Listen with your heart, listen-with your mind, when you really listen, love is what you'll find.

I'm here to make you laugh, so while I'm talking, think of something funny.

When you are older, you have greater knowledge, you have had more experience, so I can use more words because you understand. I do not suffer from LOGOKAPHOSIS (inability to understand spoken directions).

You can't have a counterfeit without a genuine.

There is no saving power by merely acknowledging a fault.

Girls that wear tight clothes have not been well reared.

The future depends on the decisions you make today.

XI

WORKING

If you don't do it now, who will do it and when will it be done?

Money may not buy happiness, but you can purchase a change of misery with it.

The best place to find helping hands is at the end of your own arms.

When we do not have to work for a living, the millennium will be here.

WORK. It doesn't take *time;* it takes *commitment.*

Some day you are going to pay a higher price.

Look for the best, dream of the best, demand the best, and work for the best, and you will get the best.

Happiness is not doing what we want, but liking what we do.

Work is love made visible.
—*Kahlil Gibran*

Nothing is of value unless it is a preparation for what is ahead.

It does not matter where we are on the mountain as long as we are going up.

The church that will not provide for temporal salvation will not provide for spiritual salvation.

You can only lift someone when you are higher than they are.

You are the kind of person on which this nation is going to lean.

I was in the bee business, but I got stung.

He had the ability to put one foot in front of the other.

The difference between good and great is a little effort.

When sacrifice is not found in the church, the church is in trouble.

Tell me what you do in your leisure, and I'll tell you what you are becoming.

When you climb a ladder, you must begin at the bottom.

Mud pots go "blub, blub"; Old Faithful goes in the air. The difference is enthusiasm.

Oh, Lord, use me, but only in an advisory capacity.

I do nothing for fear of making a mistake.

In case the Lord needs help, bring your shovel.

Build bridges and tear down the wall.

If all the protesters were producers, this world would be different.

We do not need unity; we demand it.

People moonlight because they don't know how to play.

Good salesmen eat fast.

It's not what you do that makes you happy, but how well you do it.

Don't depend on others for happiness.

What would the church songs sound like if we changed all the *work* words to *play* words. *Play* while the sun is radiant. *Play* for the night draws nigh. Joy has more meaning than *play*. 'Tis noble of man to *play* and to give. I have play enough to do. We will *play* out our salvation. How sweet the *play*, my God, my King. Today while the sun shines, *play* with a will.

We do not learn by defining but by experiencing.

Where much is given much is required.

There is only one way to make money. What's that? I knew you would not know.

Two frogs fell in a churn. One gave up: the other kicked till he churned the butter and hopped out.

Man's reach should exceed his grasp.

Accept the challenge free time offers you. We live in the world we have created.

Your heaviest burden is when you have nothing to carry.

The Lord sent us here, but we have to earn our way back.

I am going to a country where the people spend all their waking hours filling their stomachs.

We do not die on the three-yard line or on third base.

The best place to spend your vacation is just inside your income.

Budget: a record of what it should have been spent for.

The best form of gambling and one that is legal is betting on yourself.

Women's slacks don't come in odd sizes; they just get that way from wear.

Money may not buy happiness, but with it you can be unhappy in comfort.

Personality is the ability to get along on banana oil instead of elbow grease.

A little more determination, a little more pluck, a little more work — that's luck.

The nicest thing about summer is it's always too hot to do the things we didn't get done last winter when it was too cold.

Lost time is never found.

You'll never get anything done by letting things slide…UNLESS YOU PLAY THE TROMBONE.

The hard part of making good is that you have to do it every day.

Those who continue to shrink from responsibility—continue to shrink.

A man tires of anything unless he earns it himself.

Build castles in the air; then put foundations under them.

No matter how good a man is, there is a better man within him.

Doing what can't be done is the joy of life.

Character building is done by piece-work.

Live through each day only. Don't try to tackle your whole life problem at once.

Any honest work is a gentleman's if performed by a gentleman.

Work is the grand cure of all the maladies and miseries that ever beset mankind. —*Thomas Carlyle*

If there were more self-starters, the boss wouldn't have to be a crank.

A hero is no braver than an ordinary man — but he is brave five minutes longer. —*Emerson*

It is incumbent upon every person of every description to contribute to his country's welfare. —*George Washington*

To get the true measure of any man's capacity, note how much more he does than is required of him.

The man who works all day, then seeks excitement at night, soon finds out something is wrong.

Emergency to a real man is simply opportunity.

We are here to add what we can to, not get what we came from, life.
—*Sir William Osler*

Most people live...in a very restricted circle of their potential being.
—*William James*

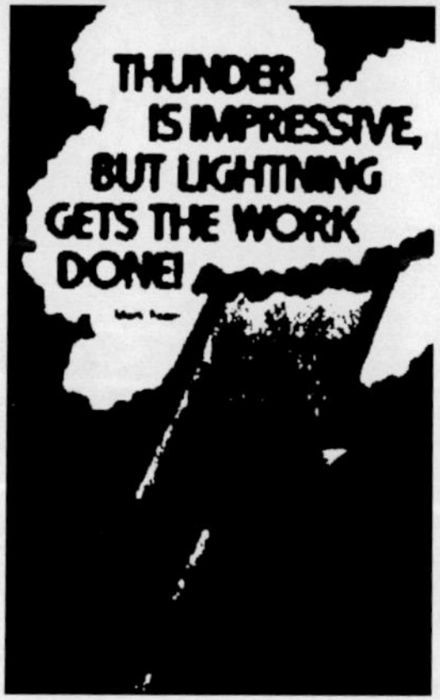

Thunder is impressive, but lightning gets the work done.
—*Mark Twain*

Nothing was ever achieved without enthusiasm.
—*Emerson*

No man can be happy unless he works for that which he has.

We must learn to do the things we do not like to do if we are to get along in this world.

Some men are too busy sawing to sharpen the saw.

There's a heap more good comes from sawin' than jawin'.

You can't work with an umbrella in one hand.

Don't hope for the best; hop for it.

If we were all satisfied, we would never reach the hill top.

The Lord hears the prayers of the hustler who prays for work.

We never know the real worth of a man or melon until they are tapped.

How you like hard work depends on whether you are doing it or paying for it.

He that does not enjoy his work is losing half his pay.

Doing nothing is the most tiresome job in the world because you can't quit and rest.

Sitting at a desk can be just as deadly as sitting in an electric chair.

When one lives above his income, there isn't much doubt about his outcome.

Life is a grindstone, and whether it grinds a man down or polishes him up depends on the stuff he is made of. —*John Billings*

The ladder of life is full of splinters, but they always prick the hardest when we are sliding down.
—William L. Brownell

Everyone can have a second car, a second house, and a TV. All it takes is a second job, a second mortgage, and a second wind.

A sign on the door of opportunity reads "Push."

Work is not particularly hard if you divide it into small parts.

A grapefruit is a lemon that had its chance and took it.

Whatever you are — be a good one.

A Hippie is a person at the bottom of the pile looking down.

We pray for mountains to be moved. What we really need is the courage to climb them.

A spectator takes no chances; he is always right.

If you are not satisfied with your lot in life, build a service station.

Good is the real enemy of the best.

Give me a kick in the can'ts.

What are you going to do with your time when you live in the Garden of Eden?

I went from a *could-be* to a *has-been* without ever being an *is*.

If you're going to leave footprints in the sands of time, you have to wear work shoes.

Use not only your brain, but your brawn as well.

The best players survive, and the casualties become spectators.

XII

OBFUSCATIONS OF CELEBRATED ORACULAR UTTERANCES

— or —

IN OTHER WORDS

1. Pulchritude possesses solely cutaneous profundity.

   Beauty is only skin deep. (But ugly goes clear to the bone.)

2. The stylus is more potent than the claymore.

   The pen is mightier than the sword.

3. It is fruitless to become lachrymose over precipitately departed lacteal fluid.

   Don't cry over spilt milk.

4. Surveillance should precede saltation.

   Look before you leap.

5. Neophyte's serendipity.

   Beginner's luck.

6. Scintillate, scintillate, asteroid minific.

   Twinkle, twinkle, little star.

7. Freedom from incrustations of grime is contiguous to rectitude.

   Cleanliness is next to Godliness.

8. It is fruitless to attempt to indoctrinate a superannuated canine with innovative maneuvers.

   You can't teach an old dog new tricks.

9. To depart from the path of rectitude is characteristic of the human species, but to be tolerant, loving and kind toward wrong-doers is God-like.

   To err is human, to forgive, divine.

10. Sorting on the part of mendicants must be interdicted.

    Beggars can't be choosers.

11. Male cadavers are incapable of yielding testimony.

    Dead man tell no tales.

12. Exclusive dedication to necessitous chores without interludes of hedonistic diversion renders John a hebetudinous fellow.

    All work and no play makes Jack a dull boy.

13. Eschew the implement of correction and vitiate the scion.

    Spare the rod and spoil the child.

14. Where there are visible vapors having their prevenience in ignited carbonaceous materials, there will be also observed conflagration.

    Where there's smoke, there's fire.

15. Abstention from any aleatory undertaking precludes a potential escalation of a lucrative nature.

    Nothing ventured, nothing gained.

16. Missiles of ligneous or oterous consistency have the potential of fracturing my osseous structure, but appellations will eternally remain innocuous.

    Sticks and stones will break my bones, but names will never hurt me.

17. My gastrointestinal satiety admonishes me that I have arrived at a state of deglutition inconsistent wit dietetic integrity.

    I'm stuffed.

18. In promulgating your esoteric cogitations and articulating your superficial sentimentalities or amicable philosophical observations, beware of platitudinous ponderosities.

    Don't use big words!

19. Compounds of hydrogen and oxygen in the proportion of two to one that are without visible movement invariably tend to flow with profundity.

    Still water runs deep.

20. A body of persons abiding in a domicile of silica combined with metallic oxides should not carelessly project small geologic specimens.

    People who live in glass houses should not throw stones.

21. Do not utter loud or passionate vocal expressions because of the accidental overturning of a receptacle containing a whitish opaque and nutritive fluid.

    Don't cry over spilt milk.

22. Where there is sufficient positive volition, a successful conclusion may usually be expected.

    Where there is a will, there is a way.

23. A superfluity of culinary experts has a tendency to disarrange the beef extract.

    Too many cooks spoil the broth.

24. Cast a stroke at the propitious moment when the silver-white metallic substance is of excessive temperature.

    Strike while the iron is hot.

25. A tremendous disturbance of the atmosphere is generally succeeded by a corresponding period of absolute tranquility.

    Calm follows a storm.

26. The customary symbol of regal power does not necessarily indicate mental tranquility.

    Uneasy lies the head that wears the crown.

27. Each mass of vapory collection suspended in the firmament has an interior decoration of metallic hue.

    Every cloud has a silver lining.

28. The canticle has achieved its definitive conclusion. However, its essential harmonic essence, resisting all natural phenomena, remains omnipresent.

    The song has ended, but the melody lingers on.

29. A short vocal utterance directed toward the individual possessing a high degree of knowledge meets adequately all the needs of the occasion.

    A word to the wise is sufficient.

30. Variation from the ordinary or common routine of experience is that which gives zest to man's cycle of existence.

    Variety is the spice of life.

31. Those who possess unusually little intellect often project themselves into situations where the winged, ethereal likenesses of men hesitate to perambulate.

    Fools rush in where angels fear to tread.

32. He who locks himself into the arms of Morpheus promptly at eventide and starts the day before it is officially announced by the rising sun excels in physical fitness, increases in economic assets, and cerebrates with remarkable efficiency.

    Early to bed, early to rise, makes a man healthy, wealthy, and wise.

33. The cognomens of those bereft of efficiency to judgment are definitely similar of the portion of their anatomy that extends from the brow to the lower extremity of the under jaw, in constantly being perceived on display in nights of prominence.

    Fools' names like fools' faces are always seen in public places.

34. The harmonious resonances circumgyrate and emanate at this point.

    The music goes 'round and 'round and comes out here.

35. A feathered biped in a gilded cage is equivalent to double that number at large.

    A bird in the hand is worth two in the bush.

36. Equine quadrupeds may indubitably be induced to approach that well-known standard of specific gravity, but not necessarily be induced to imbibe thereof.

    You can lead a horse to water, but you can't make him drink.

37. Calculus concretion in rotary transition gleans slight bryophitic accretion.

    A rolling stone gathers no moss.

38. The incontinently stirring rasorial vertebrae apprehends the lytta-like vermicular invertebrate.

    The early bird catches the worm.

39. It hath been deemed unwise to calculate upon the quantity of Junior poultry prior to the completion of proper incubation.

Don't count your chickens before they hatch.

40. Unwanted egotism prophesies the speedy effect of the force of gravity.

    Pride goeth before the fall.

41. The placement of the termination as a precedent to the commencement should never be essayed.

    Don't place the cart before the horse.

42. A vessel under constant optical supervision is hesitant to attain the desired temperature of 100 degrees Centigrade.

    A watched pot never boils.

43. A canine who expresses his feelings vociferously refrains from using his bicuspid maliciously.

    A barking dog never bites.

44. A small, one-eyed steel instrument used at the crucial moment may rescue the square of three.

    A stitch in time saves nine.

45. Accelerated execution often produces faulty results.

    Haste makes waste.

46. History records painful occurrences between the drinking vessel and the facial aperture which it wishes to contact.

There's many a slip 'twixt the cup and the lip.

47. Plumaged bipeds of the same genus and species assemble in multitudes.

Birds of a feather flock together.

48. When the humidity attains the bursting point, it does so profusely.

When it rains, it pours.

49. When the feline quadruped is conspicuous by its absence, the lesser rodents avail themselves of the opportunity to participate in some unrestrained frivolity.

When the cat's away, the mice will play.

50. Do not traverse a structure erected to afford passage over a waterway prior to the time of drawing nigh the same.

Don't cross the bridge before you get to it.

51. The act of impartially giving one thing an equivalent for another is not considered unlawful.

Fair exchange is no robbery.

52. Pedal habiliments of variegated hue and design articuli lubricated and illuminated with ambidextrous facility for the infinitesimal remuneration of ten cents per operation.

Shoe shine — 10 cents.

53. Permanently absented in simultaneous conjunction with severely agitated admixtures of nitrogen and oxygen.

Gone with the wind.

54. Behold, and become cognizant of the audacity and eccentricity of nature's preposterous phenomenal behavior, for the solidified atmospheric precipitation has begun and is now distilling that crystalline immaculate substance of frost upon the terra firma. Not being parsimonious with my elaborate vocabulary, it might be well to render this fastidious enigmatical expression comprehensible by mere elucidating.

It has its nerve to snow!

55. One should hyperstatically exercise micrography on that situs which one should eventually tenant should one propel oneself into the troposphere.

Look before you leap.

56. Do not dissipate your competence by habitudenous prodigality lest you subsequently lament on exiguous inadequacy.

Waste not, want not.

57. A combubiation of the correlaculorum and an itching sensation of the heart that can't be scratched.

    In love.

58. When the domesticated feline went upon nocturnal peregrinations, the miniature rodent rioted hilariously in the erstwhile unprotected domicile.

    When the cat's away, the mice will play.

Biography

Saved by Failure: The Alma Heaton Story

by: Tami Gibbons

If Alma Heaton had not failed so many times, at so many jobs, he would have never discovered his enthusiasm and love for recreation and he would never have become the legend that he is today.

"Early in life I tried farming, sheep herding, contracting, trucking, saw milling, movies, mining, cowpunching, and rodeo work," said Alma. "My performance in all of them was poor. I failed. I lost all my father's savings. I was a genuine flop. I even failed all of my high school classes except for Physical Education. At times I thought I might as well have been in the grave for all the good I did for myself or anybody else."

However, in spite of those failures, or (according to Alma) because of them, Alma is today a world leader in the field of recreation, dance, and social activity. He has created what has been called the "funnest backyard in America" and has danced his way around the world "throwing parties" and teaching others the joy of dance and recreation. In fact, Alma likes to joke that in the process of teaching dance he has had his arms around more women then any other man in history. He estimates the number is over 100,000.

The path toward a lifetime of recreation started for Alma after he was released from the Army and couldn't find a job. One of his friends suggested that he go to dance school since the Army paid ex-soldiers to go to school. The regulations did not specify what kind of school.

As a result of his dancing lessons Alma began teaching at a local dance studio and shortly afterwards began attending Weber State College.

At the time Alma did not consider it a possibility that he could simply study dance or recreation; degree programs in such disciplines simply did not exist. Yet he did not know what he wanted to study, and memories of high school failures weighed on him. His advisor, however, told him he was mechanically-minded. So he took auto mechanics—and failed it. The next quarter he took machine shop and the next the welding shop. He botched them both. The last quarter the school finally put him in refrigeration (putting poison gas into refrigeration cooling systems). That ended the day he put in a surplus of gas that not only sent all the students and teachers bolting, but killed all the trees around the building.

Alma did not give up. The next year he went to Utah State University in Logan determined that he would somehow make a living working not with things—but with people. He had noticed his brother had a lot of fun teaching recreation and that's how he wanted to make his living too—by having fun.

So, Alma decided to follow in his brother's footsteps and subsequently earned a bachelors and then masters degree in Recreation and Physical Education.

Upon graduation Alma still had difficulty finding employment until his sister-in-law was able to get him a job teaching a sixth grade class in Ogden. It was not what he had been trained for and his high school failures immediately returned to haunt him. There were numerous subjects that he simply did not know how to teach.

"One day I was to teach my students a mathematics problem involving percentages. I didn't know how to teach percentages. So I said 'push your chairs back and we'll dance.' I found so many subjects I taught badly that I spent most of my time dancing and playing games with my students."

However, once again Alma's "failure" as an elementary teacher nudged him towards his destiny because his students became so proficient in dancing and loved it so much that Dr. Charles J. Hart of BYU heard of Alma's work and asked him to teach at BYU.

His first year at BYU Alma taught tennis, handball and football. He had no previous experience in such sports. The second year he asked if he could teach dance instead, and he was given permission. Alma inaugurated the dance department at BYU.

Alma taught social, square dance, round, folk dance and elementary rhythms. He says the students didn't have to change clothes for dance class and it counted as a P.E. credit so they all wanted to take dance. "There were 5,000 students at BYU and 5,000 enrollments in dance class (some of them took four or five classes). Thirty new teachers had to be hired."

Alma also started a family recreation class, a social recreation class and a philosophy of recreation class.

Finally, after all those years, he had found a job that he could do well, a job that he loved.

Three years later Alma went to Indiana University to get a Doctorate degree. However, failure begot success again, because he did so poorly on his entrance exams that he decided the extra salary was not worth wasting three years doing something he did badly. He now knew he could make a living at something he enjoyed and in which he was a success.

Alma was not only the first professor of recreation and dance at BYU but also served on the MIA General Board for 15 years, was the first Vice President of Recreation in Utah and served on the American Association of Health, Recreation and Physical Education. (He was the only man on the board—serving with 25 women. They had nominated and voted him into the association because they thought Alma was a woman's name!)

As a result of this calling and his ability to entertain and teach, Alma and his wife Marie started traveling across America, teaching dance and social activity (they call it "throwing a party") for stake, youth and other groups. Alma's parties not only consisted of recreation, leadership, and dance instruction but a variety of other activities as well.

"I learned hundreds of poems and riddles and jokes while I was driving a truck [another of his jobs that turned into a failure: he crashed]. I would put them on cards and memorize them as I drove. Those have saved me and helped me to entertain groups."

Often at the start of a "party" Alma will form two big circles, one of girls and the other of boys and will have them march around facing each other. Than every few seconds the music will stop and the two facing each other will have to converse on whatever subject Alma shouts out (ie. "why I'm smarter than you"). Alma says he does this to teach people "the art of conversation," He says this art was lost with the creation of rock music, which he feels has led to one of the lowest and saddest forms of dance in existence.

"It's a four-legged stool dance. Every week you dance the same four beats of music with the same girl for four hours. We used to go to dances to fall in love. Rock music, however, is so loud you would not even be able to hear such words."

One time Earnest Wilkinson, the President of BYU, asked Alma to show the Prophet and Twelve Apostles what was taking place in the cultural halls of the church (this was after rock music had become all the kids danced to). He did. He picked 12 of the best "rock" dancers, went into the room with the Twelve and put on the music as loud as he could and turned the kids loose.

"President Joseph Fielding Smith never cracked a smile, but Brother Thomas Monson and some of the others were cracking smiles because these kids were just wearing their clothes out from the inside, just wiggling around like worms."

Alma will often end one of his parties by having everyone hold hands and sing "I Am a Child of God." He will then have them repeat the words, "I love you" three times and then the boys have to prove it to every girl by saying the words and giving each one a hug.

"I've never had any objections about that activity. Some girls never get to feel loved, so this way they get a hug and get to hear the three most important words there are."

In addition to teaching recreation and dance to school and community groups, Alma and his wife Marie served an 18 month church mission in India and as well as a three month mission in which they traveled to six different countries and hosted 90 different 'parties' in 90 nights, every night in a different place.

When Alma was younger he also served a mission to Canada. He says the only baptisms he had there came because one day when they were knocking on doors a little girl was having a party and invited them in. They sat down with the kids and played games with them. The mother was so impressed she invited them back.

Not only is Alma distinguished for his success in recreation and dance, but he loves games—of all sorts. In fact he has turned his backyard into a small amusement park.

In his backyard he has designed a large tree house. From the tree house visitors can rocket down a zip line on a steering wheel attached to a pulley and cable; slide down a fireman's pole; swing on a Tarzan swing; or take great leaps while suspended from elastic ropes. They can play volleyball, tether ball, wiffleball, kickball, or a variety of other games.

Alma also has two trailers in which he stores games. Those games consist of such activities as "snowballs" made of old, clean socks filled with other socks, tennis balls with long elastic bands, bean bags that are thrown through plywood targets with faces painted on them, 15-foot stationary pogo poles...the list goes on and on.

Alma says learning how to play and recreate in our leisure time is one of the most important lessons we can learn in life. Alma mentions a quote that says 'I am what I am when I do what I do when I have nothing to do.'

"Recreation is necessary because it is the foundation of civilization, it is the source of greatest happiness, it is a countersign of friendship and it is one of the best socializers. Everyone can dance. It is a universal language."

Alma certainly lives what he preaches. He is always "recreating" in his free time. He says he is always involved in about five projects. He is currently writing a book (he has written one a year for the past 50 years), recycling broken materials into games, serving as the stake Sunday School President, teaching part time at BYU, and throwing about one "party" a week.

"If you love life, don't waste time, 'cause that's what life is made of. And oh! Life has been good to me! What a change from the poor little boy raised in Kanab—it's a miracle what I've turned out to be. The Lord has saved and changed and directed my road. People can come to my back yard and play volleyball, tether ball, wiffleball, kickball, or a variety of other games.

If Alma had three wishes he says he would not be able to use them. "I couldn't wish for one more thing than I've got. I'm living where I want to; I'm teaching what I want; I have the family I want. Everything is just perfect. I couldn't ask for one more thing. That's how the Lord has blessed me."